Psychological Type Indicator (PTI)

Answer Sheet

Name

Instructions

Read each item in the accompanying booklet carefully. After you choose one of the alternative answers (A or B), place an "X" on the appropriate side of the oval in the table to the right. If you make a mistake, circle the incorrect answer and place an "X" on the correct side of the oval. Please make sure you complete all the items.

1 A B	2 A B	3 A B	4 A B
5 A B	6 A B	7 A B	8 A B
9 A B	10 A B	11 A B	12 A B
13 A B	14 A B	15 A B	16 A B
17 A B	18 A B	19 A B	20 A B
21 A B	22 A B	23 A B	24 A B
25 A B	26 A B	27 A B	28 A B
29 A B	30 A B	31 A B	32 A B
33 A B	34 A B	35 A B	36 A B
37 A B	38 A B	39 A B	40 A B
41 A B	42 A B	43 A B	44 A B
45 A B	46 A B	47 A B	48 A B
49 A B	50 A B	51 A B	52 A B
53 A B	54 A B	55 A B	56 A B

57 A B	58 A B	59 A B	60 A B
61 A B	62 A B	63 A B	64 A B
65 A B	66 A B	67 A B	68 A B
69 A B	70 A B	71 A B	72 A B
73 A B	74 A B	75 A B	76 A B
77 A B	78 A B	79 A B	80 A B
81 A B	82 A B	83 A B	84 A B
85 A B	86 A B	87 A B	88 A B
89 A B	90 A B	91 A B	92 A B
93 A B	94 A B	95 A B	96 A B
97 A B	98 A B	99 A B	100 A B
101 A B	102 A B	103 A B	104 A B
105 A B	106 A B	107 A B	108 A B
109 A B	110 A B	111 A B	112 A B
113 A B	114 A B	115 A B	116 A B

PTI

Psychological Type Indicator

QUESTIONNAIRE & INTERPRETIVE BOOKLET

ISTJ	ISFJ	INFJ	INTJ
ISTP	ISFP	INFP	INTP
ESTP	ESFP	ENFP	ENTP
ESTJ	ESFJ	ENFJ	ENTJ

HRD Press, Inc. • Amherst • Massachusetts

Published by: HRD Press, Inc.
22 Amherst Road
Amherst, MA 01002
(800) 822-2801 (U.S. and Canada)
(413) 253-3488
(413) 253-3490 (Fax)
http://www.hrdpress.com

ISBN: 0-87425-819-7

Cover design by Eileen Klockars
Production services by Anctil Virtual Office
Editorial services by Sally Farnham

Psychological Type Indicator (PTI)
Part One—The Questionnaire

Psychological Type Indicator (PTI)

Instructions

This is a questionnaire, not a test. There are no right or wrong answers. After completing this questionnaire, you will have a better understanding of how you prefer to look at things and how you go about making decisions. Although this questionnaire is about your "true self," wherever you can, focus on how you think and act in the workplace as much as possible.

On the following pages, you will find 116 items. There are two types of items. For the first 56 items (Section A), you must indicate which one of two given words appeals to you more. Base your answers only on the meaning of each word. For the remaining 60 items (Section B), you must indicate which one of two given statements more closely resembles the way you behave or would prefer to behave.

Remember
Read each item carefully, make your choice, and ensure that you mark an "X" on the appropriate side of the oval on the Answer Sheet. If you make a mistake, circle the incorrect answer and place an "X" on the correct side of the oval.

This is not a test and there is no time limit. However, it is best to work through the items as quickly as you can. Do not deliberate over any one item; your first response will tend to be the best one. The 116 items should take approximately 20 minutes to complete and you must answer all the items.

If you are not sure of what you need to do, re-read the instructions above. You may turn the page and begin once you fully understand the instructions.

Section A

For each item, choose one word from the two given words that appeals to you more in terms of meaning.

1.	(A) Outgoing	(B) Reserved
2.	(A) Certainty	(B) Chance
3.	(A) Analyze	(B) Feel
4.	(A) Careful	(B) Carefree
5.	(A) Expressive	(B) Concealing
6.	(A) Conceptual	(B) Factual
7.	(A) Tender-Minded	(B) Tough-Minded
8.	(A) Easygoing	(B) Conventional
9.	(A) Quiet	(B) Loud
10.	(A) Details	(B) Patterns
11.	(A) Logical	(B) Sentimental
12.	(A) Informal	(B) Methodical
13.	(A) Demonstrative	(B) Inhibited
14.	(A) Conceive	(B) Construct
15.	(A) Emotional	(B) Reasoned
16.	(A) Scheduled	(B) Open-Ended
17.	(A) Sociable	(B) Modest
18.	(A) Speculative	(B) Established
19.	(A) Judge	(B) Sympathize
20.	(A) Possibility	(B) Certainty

For each item, choose one word from the two given words that appeals to you more in terms of meaning.

21.	(A) Still	(B) Mobile
22.	(A) Make	(B) Invent
23.	(A) People	(B) Thoughts
24.	(A) Stability	(B) Change
25.	(A) Roused	(B) Subdued
26.	(A) Question	(B) Accept
27.	(A) Objective	(B) Subjective
28.	(A) Unrestrained	(B) Orderly
29.	(A) Reticent	(B) Forward
30.	(A) Facts	(B) Inventions
31.	(A) Discuss	(B) Agree
32.	(A) Casual	(B) Formal
33.	(A) Calm	(B) Excited
34.	(A) Abstract	(B) Real
35.	(A) Heart	(B) Head
36.	(A) Systematic	(B) Unsystematic
37.	(A) Revealing	(B) Secretive
38.	(A) Imaginary	(B) Concrete
39.	(A) Merciful	(B) Just
40.	(A) Flexible	(B) Firm
41.	(A) Expansive	(B) Understated

For each item, choose one word from the two given words that appeals to you more in terms of meaning.

42.	(A) Literal	(B) Theoretical
43.	(A) Uncritical	(B) Judgmental
44.	(A) Adventurous	(B) Organized
45.	(A) Private	(B) Public
46.	(A) Actual	(B) Potential
47.	(A) Reminisce	(B) Forecast
48.	(A) Planned	(B) Unplanned
49.	(A) Detached	(B) Engaged
50.	(A) Future	(B) Present
51.	(A) Hard	(B) Smooth
52.	(A) Spontaneous	(B) Arranged
53.	(A) Internal	(B) External
54.	(A) Statement	(B) Hypothesis
55.	(A) Fair	(B) Kind
56.	(A) Decisive	(B) Undecided

Section A concluded.

Continue to Section B.

Section B

For each item, choose the answer that more closely resembles the way you behave or would prefer to behave from the two given answers.

57. When you are at a social event, do you . . .
    (A) tend to get very involved in enjoying yourself?
    (B) stand back and watch others enjoying themselves?

58. Which of these do you consider to be more important in making decisions?
    (A) your experience
    (B) your imagination

59. When you make decisions, do you . . .
    (A) tend to use a logical approach?
    (B) let your feelings influence your decision?

60. Do you . . .
    (A) tend to make decisions too quickly?
    (B) have trouble making decisions?

61. Do you find it . . .
    (A) difficult to start conversations?
    (B) easy to initiate conversations with strangers?

62. Which of these are you more likely to be seen as?
    (A) an imaginative person
    (B) a practical person

63. Do you tend to . . .
    (A) look at the effect your actions have on others?
    (B) look at the logical consequences of your actions?

64. Do you think that the daily routine . . .
    (A) makes it easier to accomplish more things?
    (B) is a boring intrusion on your life?

65. Do you . . .
    (A) often act without thinking?
    (B) often think about things without acting on them?

66. Which of these do you prefer to deal with?
    (A) a problem requiring a theoretical solution
    (B) a problem requiring a real-life solution

67. With regard to career choice, would you prefer . . .
    (A) a job that involves working with people?
    (B) a job that involves working with concepts and theories?

68. Do you consider yourself . . .
    (A) an impulsive person?
    (B) someone who considers all the options first?

69. Are you . . .
    (A) more at home in the world of people?
    (B) more at home in the world of ideas?

70. When choosing a book to read, do you prefer . . .
    (A) a work of nonfiction?
    (B) a work of fiction?

71. Which is it better to be?
    (A) somewhat insensitive to the needs of others
    (B) more concerned for others' needs than your own

72. Do you . . .
    (A) prefer to prepare for events well in advance?
    (B) think it's best to leave things open?

73. When you have news, do you tend to . . .
    (A) keep things to yourself?
    (B) let a lot of other people know?

74. Do you prefer to take in information . . .
    (A) as one "big picture"?
    (B) on a step-by-step basis?

75. When arguing a point, do you . . .
    (A) try to convince people with the sentiment of your argument?
    (B) try to convince people with the structure of your argument?

76. Do you find that you . . .
    (A) enjoy the exhilaration from last-minute pressures?
    (B) try to avoid any last-minute pressures?

77. Are you . . .
    (A) often impatient when working on long drawn-out jobs?
    (B) usually unphased working on the same project for a long time?

78. Would you say that . . .
    (A) you are oriented toward the future?
    (B) you are oriented toward the present?

79. Would you prefer to be seen as . . .
    (A) someone who uses logic to solve problems?
    (B) someone who considers feelings when solving problems?

80. Do you prefer to . . .
    (A) do things spontaneously?
    (B) follow a set schedule?

81. When communicating with others, do you prefer to . . .
    (A) talk to them on the phone?
    (B) send an e-mail to them?

82. Are you more concerned with . . .
    (A) theories and beliefs?
    (B) immediate interests and issues?

83. Do you prefer to . . .
    (A) actually observe the truth personally?
    (B) observe the truth objectively?

84. When tackling a project, do you . . .
    (A) plan each step before you start?
    (B) deal with the issues as they arise?

85. When studying something new, do you find it easier to learn . . .
    (A) when studying by yourself?
    (B) when working in a study group with other people?

86. Are you . . .
    (A) more interested in practical issues?
    (B) more interested in conceptual matters?

87. Do you . . .
    (A) find it easy to give criticism when necessary?
    (B) avoid being critical of others even when criticism may be required?

88. If someone asked you what you will be doing next Sunday, would you . . .
    (A) have nothing definite planned?
    (B) know exactly what you would be doing?

89. Would you describe yourself as . . .
    (A) someone with lots of friends?
    (B) someone with a few close friends?

90. Are you the type of person who . . .
    (A) tends to trust their intuition?
    (B) tends to question their intuition?

91. Which do you consider worse?
    (A) a person who is not sympathetic enough
    (B) a person who is overly sympathetic

92. Do you usually arrive at meetings . . .
    (A) on time or sometimes slightly late?
    (B) on time or often early?

93. Do you think others find it . . .
    (A) difficult to get to know you?
    (B) easy to get to know you?

94. Which would you prefer people to approach you for?
    (A) workable solutions to real problems
    (B) new ideas

95. Do you prefer to be seen as . . .
    (A) a firm-minded, logical individual?
    (B) a tender-minded, sympathetic individual?

96. Which of these do you find hardest?
    (A) adapting to routine
    (B) dealing with constant change

97. Would you prefer to . . .
    (A) read a good book?
    (B) go to a party?

98. Do you think it is better to . . .
    (A) find innovative ways of tackling tasks?
    (B) stick to tried and tested ways of doing things?

99. At work, do you . . .
    (A) try to please as many people as possible?
    (B) often hurt people's feelings without knowing it?

100. Do you prefer to focus on . . .
   (A) the process of a project?
   (B) the completion of a project?

101. Do you get . . .
   (A) more excited than most people?
   (B) less excited than most people?

102. Are you . . .
   (A) more concerned with details?
   (B) more concerned with the overall picture?

103. Which of these do you consider to be your greater strength?
   (A) your ability to solve problems
   (B) your ability to understand other people

104. Do you like to . . .
   (A) organize things in advance?
   (B) be as flexible as possible?

105. With regards to your interests, do you think you have . . .
   (A) a few to which you can devote more time?
   (B) a lot that you devote a little time to each?

106. Are you more likely to see yourself as someone who . . .
   (A) questions traditional methods of doing things?
   (B) adjusts to traditional methods of doing things?

107. Do you tend to . . .
   (A) prefer to make "clever" decisions?
   (B) prefer to make people happy?

108. When going on vacations, do you . . .
   (A) plan what you want to see and do?
   (B) see what each day brings?

109. At parties, are you . . .
   (A) sociable and outgoing?
   (B) somewhat quiet and reserved?

110. Do you . . .
   (A) prefer to use established procedures?
   (B) like to find new ways of doing things?

111. Do you feel most rewarded when . . .
   (A) other people's needs are met?
   (B) a job is done well?

112. Do you enjoy . . .
   (A) a flexible approach to your work?
   (B) a planned approach to your work?

113. Do you find it easier to . . .
   (A) follow the lead of others?
   (B) take the lead yourself?

114. Which of these do you enjoy most?
   (A) learning new skills
   (B) applying skills you have already learned

115. When evaluating a situation, do you . . .
   (A) use objective reasoning?
   (B) prefer to be guided by your own values and beliefs?

116. When things are changing quickly, do you . . .
   (A) find it easy to adapt to the new situation?
   (B) find change a bit disconcerting?

Section B concluded.

End of assessment; follow the scoring instructions on your Answer Sheet.

Psychological Type Indicator (PTI)
Part Two—Interpretive Material

Introduction

The Background to Psychological Type

One of the earliest known theories of human typology is from the Greek philosopher Hippocrates who proposed four fundamental types of sanguine (happy), choleric (irritable), melancholic (sad), and phlegmatic (calm). Many other personality characteristics or behaviors have been further drawn out from these four temperaments, although the premise of the four temperaments has been relatively enduring through the ages. Carl Jung, an early student of Sigmund Freud, was perhaps the greatest proponent of typological personality theory, and classified personality into eight types. Numerous other type theories have been proposed but none has been so successfully applied and scientifically accepted as Jungian type theory.

Type indicator questionnaires (such as the MBTI®, JTI, and PTI), based on Jung's psychology, have been designed to measure the attitudes and functions of the individual's personality in order to determine their personality type based on these four dimensions. The four tiers or dimensions of personality are:

Preferences		Process
Extroversion (E)	Introversion (I)	Attitude
Sensing (S)	Intuition (N)	Function
Thinking (T)	Feeling (F)	Function
Judging (J)	Perceiving (P)	Attitude

Each of the four preferences is symbolized by its first letter (except for iNtuition, which is symbolized by the letter "N" to avoid confusing it with Introversion). The combination of the four preferences gives a possible 16 combinations of personality type, e.g., ESTP, INFJ, ENFP, etc.

The Psychological Type Indicator (PTI) is an assessment of Jungian Type that has been designed to help individuals find the type that most closely matches their preferences.

This booklet seeks to provide some summary feedback based on the results of your PTI.

General Type Preference Descriptors

The following information offers a brief summary of Jung's psychological type theory. Jung suggested that there are four preferences:

- **Either Extroversion (E) or Introversion (I)**
  Our energy orientation toward the world around us *(attitude).*

  Extroverts relate more easily to the world of people, things, and events outside of themselves. They tend to be more outgoing, active, and responsive to their environment.

  Introverts relate more easily to the ideas and concepts in their mind. They are focused on subjective experiences that are viewed individually.

- **Either Sensing (S) or Intuition (N)**
  Two different ways in which we perceive and gather information *(function).*

  When you are perceiving with your Sensing process, you are interested in what your five senses show you—what exists in the present. Information perceived is taken as given, and reality of experiences is appreciated.

  When you are perceiving with your Intuition, you are using your imagination to see new possibilities and insights hidden from the senses. Intuition is an unconscious process that looks to explore and gain new insights.

- **Either Thinking (T) or Feeling (F)**
  Two ways in which we make judgments and decisions *(function).*

  When you make judgments with your Thinking, you base your decisions on impersonal analysis and logic. Thinking types focus on facts and are less concerned with feelings, or can ignore emotions.

  When you make your judgments with your Feeling, you base your decisions on your values. Feeling types operate best when they can develop relationships and share feelings. They act according to values such as seeking harmony, satisfaction, and emotional well-being.

- **Either Judging (J) or Perceiving (P)**
  Two ways of living in the world around us *(attitude).*

  When you are living by your Judgment, you like to have things decided; your life is likely to be planned and orderly. Life is more regulated and events prepared.

  When you are living by your Perception, you do not want to miss anything; your way of life is likely to be spontaneous and flexible. Opportunity for new experience and being able to adapt to changing circumstances are sources of stimulation to the Perceiving type.

Key Descriptors for Each Preference

A description of each preference and typical behaviors of each type are given below.

The Attitudes

Introversion	Extroversion
• Prefer reflection • Prefer to write more than talk • Enjoy social contact, but need to recover from it • Want to understand something before trying it • Persistent • Like a quiet space to work in	• Prefer action • Talk readily • Want to experience things in order to understand • Gain energy from others • Like variety • Work by trial and error

Judging	Perceiving
• Decisive • Industrious and determined • Organized and systematic • Uneasy about unplanned happenings • Take deadlines seriously • Like to have things decided and settled	• Curious • Flexible and tolerant • Leave things open • Pull things together well at the last minute • Expect to find new experiences interesting • Sample many more experiences than can be digested or used

The Functions

Sensing	Intuition
• Like facts • Realistic and practical • Observant about what is actually happening • Work steadily and step-by-step • Enjoy owning things and making them work • Patient and good with detail	• See patterns and possibilities • Imaginative, speculative • Like to see the overall picture • Work in bursts of energy with quiet periods in between (need inspiration) • Like variety • Impatient with routine

Thinking	Feeling
• Fair, firm minded, and skeptical • Like to use reason and objectivity • Brief and businesslike • Analytical and logical • Critical • Clear and consistent principles	• Warm, sympathetic, aware of how others feel • Trusting • Enjoy pleasing others • Need harmony • Will often avoid conflict • Clear and consistent values

Summary Descriptions of the 16 Personality Types

ISTJ ISTJs prefer dealing with facts, and making decisions after considering the various options. They organize their life on a logical basis. They are quiet, serious, and well prepared for most eventualities. They are keen observers of life, developing good understanding of situations, which is often not expressed. They have a strong sense of practical objectives and work efficiently to meet them.	**ISFJ** ISFJs prefer dealing with facts and people, and making decisions on the basis of personal values. Their lives are organized on a personal basis, seeking to enjoy relationships with people they like. They are quiet, serious observers of people, and are both conscientious and loyal. They prefer work that involves being of practical service to people. They are often concerned for and perceptive of how other people feel, and dislike confrontation and conflict.	**INFJ** INFJs take their energy from the inner world of thoughts and emotions. They prefer dealing with patterns and possibilities, particularly for people, and they make decisions using personal values. Their lives are organized on a personal basis. They often have a private sense of purpose in life, and work steadily to fulfill that goal. They demonstrate a quiet concern for people, being interested in helping them to develop and grow. They are good at developing insight into people, though it can often remain unexpressed.	**INTJ** INTJs prefer dealing with patterns and possibilities for the future, and making decisions using impersonal analysis. Their lives are organized on a logical basis. They are strategists, identifying long-term goals and organizing life to meet them. They tend to be skeptical and critical, both of self and others, with a keen sense of deficiencies in quality and competence. They often have strong intellects, yet are able to attend to details that are relevant to the strategy.
ISTP ISTPs prefer dealing with facts and making decisions on a logical basis. Their lives are flexible, demonstrating an interest in acquiring new information that leads to a practical understanding of the way the world works. They are quiet and detached, and adaptable (up to a point). They are often good at solving organizational problems that need to be thought through. They are curious about how and why things work, and can seem impulsive, sometimes producing surprising ideas or doing something unpredictable.	**ISFP** ISFPs prefer dealing with facts and people, and making decisions on the basis of personal values. They are adaptable (up to a point), quiet, and friendly. They are interested in people, enjoying their company, preferably on an individual basis or in small numbers. They take a caring and sensitive approach to helping others. They enjoy the present and tend to dislike confrontation and conflict. They usually act as very supportive members of a team.	**INFP** INFPs prefer dealing with patterns and possibilities, especially for people, and prefer to make decisions on the basis of personal values. Their lives are flexible, following new insights and possibilities as they arise. They are quiet and adaptable (up to a point—when their values are violated the normally adaptable INFPs can surprise people with their stance). They will seem to be interested in ideas, and they may sometimes make creative contributions. They have a hidden warmth for people, and a desire to see self and others grow and develop. They prefer to undertake work that has a meaningful purpose.	**INTP** INTPs prefer dealing with patterns and possibilities, and making decisions on a logical basis. Their lives are flexible, following new insights and possibilities as they arise. They are quiet and detached, and adaptable (up to a point—sometimes they may stop adapting, insisting that there is a clear principle at stake). They are not interested in routine, and will often experiment or change things to see if they can be improved. They operate at their best when solving complex problems that require the application of intellect.
ESTP ESTPs prefer dealing with facts, which they usually view objectively, and they make decisions on a logical basis. Their lives are flexible, consisting of a series of activities that interest them. They are action-oriented problem solvers, and prefer to work with practical organizational issues. They can be impulsive, and like taking part in trouble-shooting–type work. They can sometimes neglect follow through, but will work best when there is a lot going on that needs organizing and solving.	**ESFP** ESFPs prefer dealing with facts, which they usually take at face value. They also prefer dealing with the present and with people, and probably derive much enjoyment out of friendships. Their lives are flexible, living very much in the present and responding to things as they arise. They are impulsive and friendly, seeking enjoyment out of life, and make new friends easily. They like taking part in solving urgent problems, such as fire fighting or trouble shooting. They operate best in practical situations involving people.	**ENFP** ENFPs prefer dealing with patterns and possibilities, particularly for people, and make decisions on the basis of personal values. Their lives are flexible, following new insights and possibilities as they arise. They are creative and insightful, often seeking to try new ideas that can be of benefit to people. They may sometimes neglect details and planning, but they enjoy work that involves experimentation and variety, working toward a general goal.	**ENTP** ENTPs prefer dealing with patterns and possibilities, and making decisions on a logical basis. They are adaptable, tending to focus on new ideas and interests as they arise, particularly if they involve increasing their competence or skill. They are often ingenious problem solvers, constantly trying new ideas out, which can make it seem as if they enjoy a good argument. They are interested in instigating change, and operate best in overcoming new difficulties where the solution requires the application of creative effort.
ESTJ ESTJs prefer dealing with facts and the present, and make decisions using logic. Their lives are organized on a logical basis. They are therefore practical, and likely to implement tried and trusted solutions to practical problems in a businesslike and impersonal manner. They prefer to ensure that the details have been taken care of rather than spend time considering concepts and strategies.	**ESFJ** ESFJs prefer dealing with facts and making decisions on the basis of personal values. They like dealing with people and organize life on a personal basis. They are usually warm people, seeking to maintain harmonious relationships with colleagues and friends who are a very important part of their lives. They can find conflict and criticism difficult to handle. They have a strong sense of duty and loyalty, and are driven by a need to belong and be of service to people.	**ENFJ** ENFJs prefer dealing with patterns and possibilities, particularly for people, and make decisions using personal values. Their lives are organized on a personal basis, seeking to develop and maintain stable relationships with those people they like. They are actively concerned with promoting personal growth in others. They are also highly sociable and expressive of feelings toward others, but can find conflict and criticism difficult, particularly if it might damage long-term relationships. They work best in situations involving people.	**ENTJ** ENTJs prefer dealing with patterns and possibilities, and making decisions after considering the consequences of the various courses of action. Their lives are organized on a logical basis. They tend to control life, organizing systems and people to meet task-oriented goals. They often take the role of executive or director, using a business-like and impersonal approach. They may appear intolerant of people who do not set high standards for themselves or don't seem to be good at what they do.

Jung's 16 Personality Types

INFJ (page 30)	**INFP** (page 33)	**ISTJ** (page 26)	**ISFJ** (page 29)
ENFJ (page 31)	**ENFP** (page 32)	**ESTJ** (page 27)	**ESFJ** (page 28)
INTJ (page 34)	**INTP** (page 37)	**ISTP** (page 22)	**ISFP** (page 25)
ENTJ (page 35)	**ENTP** (page 36)	**ESTP** (page 23)	**ESFP** (page 24)

The following pages contain a one-page summary of each of the 16 different types. Find your type on the chart above, and turn to the page number listed.

An 8-page *TypeBook* for each of the different types is available for $4.95 from HRD Press, Inc. Each of these booklets covers:

- How to communicate with this type
- Contributions of this type to a team
- Career preferences for this type
- Signs of stress in this type
- Time management for this type
- Conflict resolution with this type
- General hints and tips for this type

An online version of the *PTI* is also available. The *PTI* Online produces a 20-page type-customized report to the user.

For more information or to order 8-page *TypeBooks* or *PTI* Online, call 1-800-822-2801 or e-mail pti@hrdpress.com.

The ISTP
Introverted Thinking aided by Sensing

Around six in one hundred people are an ISTP type. ISTPs have a compelling drive to understand the way things work. They're good at logical analysis and like to use it on practical concerns. They typically have strong powers of reasoning, although they're not interested in theories or concepts unless they can see a practical application. They like to take things apart and see the way they work.

ISTPs typically have an adventuresome spirit. They thrive on action and are often fearless. ISTPs are fiercely independent, needing to have the space to make their own decisions about their next step. They do not necessarily believe in or follow rules and regulations, as this would prohibit their ability to "do their own thing." Their sense of adventure and desire for constant action make ISTPs prone to becoming bored rather quickly.

ISTPs are generally loyal to their causes and beliefs, and are firm believers that people should be treated with equity and fairness. Although they do not respect the rules of the "System," they faithfully follow their own rules and guidelines for behavior. They like and need to spend time alone, because this is when they can sort things out in their minds most clearly. They absorb large quantities of impersonal facts from the external world, and sort through those facts, making judgments, when they are alone.

What Makes an ISTP Tick?

The dominant function is the judging one of Thinking. Characteristics associated with this function include the following:

- Likes making decisions on the basis of logic, using objective considerations
- Is concerned with truth, principles, and justice
- Is analytical and critical, tending to see the flaws in situations
- Takes an objective approach

The judging Thinking function is introverted. That is, Thinking is used primarily to govern the inner world of thoughts and emotions. The ISTP will therefore:

- Spend time thinking analytically, organizing thoughts on a logical basis
- Develop an understanding of the principles involved in a situation
- Spontaneously feel critical of a person or situation, but not necessarily express that criticism
- Be inwardly decisive, but not communicate those decisions to others
- Think mostly about impersonal issues, focusing more on concepts, truths, and systems rather than individuals' feelings

The Thinking function is primarily supported by the extroverted Sensing perception—the Sensing perception is used primarily to manage the outer world of actions and spoken words. This will modify the way that the Thinking is directed by:

- Focusing the Thinking (inner world) on understanding practical or mechanical problems
- Perceiving appropriate facts to support the logical analysis

The classic temperament of an ISTP is Dionysian, or Sanguine, for whom freedom is a basic driving force—seeking to enjoy the present.

The ESTP
Extroverted Sensing aided by Thinking

ESTPs are men and women of action. When someone of this type is present, things begin to happen. The lights come on, the music plays, the game begins. And a game it is for the ESTP: the natural entrepreneur, the diplomat, the conciliator, and the negotiator par excellence. Approximately 8% of the general population are of this extroverted, sensing, thinking, perceiving type, and if only one adjective could be used to describe ESTPs, *resourceful* would be an apt choice.

Life is never dull around ESTPs. Their friendly style often has a theatrical flourish that makes even the most routine, mundane event seem exciting at times.

ESTPs can be almost uncanny at observing people's motivations, being somehow hypersensitive to even the most minimal of nonverbal cues, which other types might miss.

What Makes an ESTP Tick?

The dominant function is the perceptive one of Sensing. Characteristics associated with this function include the following:

- Likes looking at information in terms of facts and details
- Focuses more on the here and now rather than possibilities for the future
- Feels comfortable in areas of proven experience
- Takes a realistic approach

The perceptive Sensing function is extroverted—Sensing is used primarily to govern the outer world of actions and spoken words. The ESTP will therefore:

- Seek to experience and enjoy the world as it is
- Be very responsive to current events, with life tending to be a succession of events
- Be pragmatic in nature, constantly seeking to change the world to the way the ESTP wants it to be
- Observe in an objective way, valuing facts without necessarily putting an interpretation on them

The Sensing function is primarily supported by introverted Thinking judgment—Thinking judgment is used primarily to manage the inner world of thoughts and emotions. This will modify the way that the Sensing is directed by:

- Focusing the Sensing (outer world) on impersonal facts and logical options
- Tending to enjoy action and events for themselves rather than for the company of others
- Leading to enjoyment of material possessions

The classic temperament of an ESTP is Dionysian, or Sanguine, for whom freedom is a basic driving force—seeking to experience and enjoy life.

The ESFP
Extroverted Sensing aided by Feeling

ESFPs radiate attractive warmth and optimism. Smooth, witty, charming, clever, voluble, and open to the environment—this describes ESFPs who, like ESTPs, represent about 10% of the population. ESFPs can be great fun to be with and are arguably the most generous of all the types. *Performer* would be the word that best describes an ESFP.

ESFPs will typically avoid being alone and seek the company of others whenever possible. ESFPs easily find company since others are usually highly entertained by the presence of an ESFP. ESFPs tend to enjoy excitement and create it wherever they are. Their joy of living is contagious and generally they wear happy faces.

What Makes an ESFP Tick?

The dominant function is the perceptive one of Sensing. Characteristics associated with this function include the following:

- Likes looking at information in terms of facts and details
- Focuses more on the here and now rather than possibilities for the future
- Feels comfortable in areas of proven experience
- Takes a realistic approach

The perceptive Sensing function is extroverted—Sensing is used primarily to govern the outer world of actions and spoken words. The ESFP will therefore:

- Seek to experience and enjoy the world as it is
- Is very responsive to current events, life tending to be a succession of events
- Be pragmatic in nature, constantly seeking to change the world to the way the ESFP wants it to be
- Observe in an objective way, valuing facts without necessarily putting an interpretation on them

The Sensing function is primarily supported by introverted Feeling judgment—Feeling judgment is used primarily to manage the inner world of thoughts and emotions. This will modify the way that the Sensing is directed by:

- Focusing the Sensing (outer world) on relationships and facts concerning people
- Tending to enjoy action and events for the company of others rather than the events themselves
- Leading to enjoyment of interaction with people

The classic temperament of an ESFP is Dionysian, or Sanguine, which seeks to be free from constraint, seeking to enjoy the present and tending to act on impulse.

The ISFP
Introverted Feeling aided by Sensing

ISFPs are found in about 6% of the general population. The best name for this type is "free spirit," because they have an intense need for freedom. Their need for social interaction, however, is not as great as that of the type they most resemble, the ESFP. An ISFP might forgo all social ties of any duration to preserve the freedom to go wherever they want.

ISFPs also resemble INFPs in needing to achieve intensity of feeling. The focus, however, with the ISFPs seems to be more on the sensuous side than the meaningful side. The ISFP is orgiastic, demanding that life provide the excitement and pleasure of drinking deeply at the Dionysian well. Not revelry (that is the forte of the ESFP) but experience is what attracts the ISFP to these kinds of activities.

ISFPs tend to be quiet and reserved, and difficult to get to know well. They hold back their ideas and opinions except from those who they are closest to. They are likely to be kind, gentle and sensitive in their dealings with others. They are interested in contributing to people's sense of well-being and happiness, and will put a great deal of effort and energy into tasks they believe in.

What Makes an ISFP Tick?

The dominant function is the judging one of Feeling. Characteristics associated with this function include the following:

- Makes decisions on the basis of personal values
- Is appreciative and accepting of people—enjoying company and seeking harmony
- Assesses the impact of decisions on others, being sympathetic or compassionate
- Takes a personal approach

The judging Feeling function is introverted—Feeling is used primarily to govern the inner world of thoughts and emotions. The ISFP will therefore:

- Develop an inner emotional life that is often unseen to others, but is experienced as intense
- Retain a strong sense of values that are often not expressed
- Emotionally accept or reject various aspects of life—for example, deciding whether praise or criticism received is valid and, at an extreme, ignoring whatever is unacceptable to him or her
- Feel appreciation toward others, but not express it

The Feeling function is primarily supported by extroverted Sensing perception—Sensing perception is used primarily to manage the outer world of actions and spoken words. This will modify the way that the Feeling is directed by:

- Focusing the Feeling (inner world) on current relationships and people (e.g., through one-to-one discussions and fact-based conversation)
- Seeking to enjoy the company of those they know, and being concerned for their well-being and happiness
- Helping people in practical ways

The classic temperament of an ISFP is Dionysian, or Sanguine, for whom freedom from constraint is a basic driving force—seeking to enjoy the present.

The ISTJ
Introverted Sensing aided by Thinking

ISTJs are characterized by decisiveness in practical affairs and are guardians of time-honored institutions. If only one adjective could be selected to describe ISTJs, it would be "dependable." ISTJs represent about 8% of the general population. An ISTJ's word is their bond.

Whether at home or at work, this type is rather quiet and serious. ISTJs are extraordinarily persevering and dependable. The thought of dishonoring a commitment would not typically occur to them. When they give their word, they give their honor.

ISTJs can be counted on to conserve the resources of the institution they serve and bring to their work a practical point of view. They perform their duties without flourish or fanfare; therefore, the dedication they bring to their work can often go unnoticed and unappreciated.

What Makes an ISTJ Tick?

The dominant function is the perceptive one of Sensing. Characteristics associated with this function include the following:

- Likes looking at information in terms of facts and details
- Focuses more on the here and now rather than possibilities for the future
- Feels comfortable in areas of proven experience
- Takes a realistic approach

The perceptive Sensing function is introverted—Sensing is used primarily to govern the inner world of thoughts and emotions. The ISTJ will therefore:

- Seek to develop a realistic understanding of the world as it is, in the light of what he/she observes
- Be pragmatic in nature, constantly learning to adapt to the world as it is now
- Observe in a subjective way, selecting and relating facts that others would not, and seeing those facts more in terms of impressions and significance than pure fact

The Sensing function is primarily supported by extroverted Thinking judgment—Thinking judgment is used primarily to manage the outer world of actions and spoken words. This will modify the way that the Sensing is directed, by:

- Focusing the Sensing (inner world) on impersonal facts and logical options
- Tending to spot flaws and injustices
- Making decisions on the basis of logical analysis that support the ISTJ's understanding of the world

The classic temperament of an ISTJ is Epimethean, or melancholic, for whom a basic driving force is duty, service, and the need to belong.

The ESTJ
Extroverted Thinking aided by Sensing

ESTJs are very much in touch with the external environment. The best adjective to describe ESTJs would be *responsible.* They represent about 13% of the general population.

ESTJs are outstanding at organizing orderly procedures and in detailing rules and regulations. They like to see things done correctly. They tend to be impatient with those who do not carry out procedures with sufficient attention to those details, prescribed by those with the most experience to get the job done right.

ESTJs are comfortable in evaluating others and tend to judge how a person is doing in terms of standard operating procedures. They might, at times, be abrupt with those who do not follow rules correctly. ESTJs are realistic, matter-of-fact, and more curious about new devices and processes than about new principles and theories.

What Makes an ESTJ Tick?

The dominant function is the judging one of Thinking. Characteristics associated with this function include the following:

- Likes making decisions on the basis of logic, using objective considerations
- Is concerned with truth, principles, and justice
- Is analytical and critical, tending to see the flaws in situations
- Takes an objective approach

The judging Thinking function is extroverted. That is, Thinking is used primarily to govern the outer world of actions and spoken words. The ESTJ will therefore:

- Organize life in a logical basis, classifying, ordering, and directing facts and situations
- Be decisive, with the aim of being just and fair
- Spontaneously criticize
- Be comfortable with conflict as a way of resolving problems
- Take an impersonal approach, focusing more on systems and organizational needs than each individual's feelings

The Thinking function is primarily supported by the introverted Sensing perception—Sensing perception is used primarily to manage the inner world of thoughts and emotions. This will modify the way that the Thinking is directed by:

- Focusing the Thinking (outer world) on practical decisions that lead to tried and trusted ways of organizing or solving problems
- Focusing decisions on immediate considerations (e.g., short-term costs and benefits, and the next step)

The classic temperament of an ESTJ is Epimethean, or melancholic, for whom a basic driving force is duty, service, and belonging.

The ESFJ
Extroverted Feeling aided by Sensing

ESFJs, possibly the most sociable of all types, are energized by interactions with people, tending to idealize whatever or whoever they admire. Harmony is a key to this type, which is represented in about 12% of the general population.

ESFJs are the great nurturers. Wherever they go, they promote harmony and harmonious relationships. They are usually able to call people correctly by name, even after one introduction. At a social gathering, they can be observed attending to the needs of others, trying to ensure that all are comfortable and involved.

ESFJs are hurt by indifference and need to be appreciated both for themselves and for the abundance, typically in the form of services, they give to others. They are conscious of appearances and take the opinions of others regarding social standards very seriously. Values in an ESFJ might take the form of should's and should not's and might be freely expressed. ESFJs can become restless when isolated from people.

What Makes an ESFJ Tick?

The dominant function is the judging one of Feeling. Characteristics associated with this function include the following:

- Makes decisions on the basis of personal values
- Is appreciative and accepting of people—enjoying company and seeking harmony
- Assesses the impact of decisions on others, being sympathetic or compassionate
- Takes a personal approach

The judging Feeling function is extroverted—Feeling is used primarily to govern the outer world of actions and spoken words. The ESFJ will therefore:

- Seek stable, harmonious relationships
- Tend to adapt to the environment, taking on board those values that are held as important by friends and family, or society as a whole
- Express the appreciation that is felt toward others
- Tend to consider others' feelings before his/her own
- Be sensitive to praise and criticism, and seek to conform to others' reasonable expectations

The Feeling function is primarily supported by introverted Sensing perception—Sensing perception is used primarily to manage the inner world of thoughts and emotions. This will modify the way that the Feeling is directed by:

- Focusing the Feeling (outer world) on current relationships and people (e.g., through social events and fact-based conversation)
- Finding practical ways to be of service to people
- Viewing people subjectively, observing facts that support harmonious relationships

The classic temperament of an ESFJ is Epimethean, or melancholic, for whom a basic driving force is duty, service and the desire to belong.

The ISFJ
Introverted Sensing aided by Feeling

Seven out of every one hundred people are ISFJs. The primary desire of ISFJs is to be of service and to provide care and nurture or to minister to individual needs. ISFJs carry a sense of history—a sense of continuity with past events and relationships. Traditions and the conservation of resources are highly valued.

The least hedonistic of all types, ISFJs believe work are intrinsically good and play must be earned. ISFJs are therefore willing to work long hours where necessary. When they undertake a task, it will be completed if at all humanly possible. Adhering to an established way of doing things and doing them well are valued and respected.

The efficiency and effectiveness of an established procedure is not often questioned. If others violate or ignore these standard and well-proven operating procedures, ISFJs are often annoyed and irritated, although they might not always display this reaction. Usually, such irritation is turned inward and may be experienced as self-absorption and fatigue.

What Makes an ISFJ Tick?

The dominant function is the perceptive one of Sensing. Characteristics associated with this function include the following:

- Likes looking at information in terms of facts and details
- Focuses more on the here and now rather than possibilities for the future
- Feels comfortable in areas of proven experience
- Takes a realistic approach

The perceptive Sensing function is introverted—Sensing is used primarily to govern the inner world of thoughts and emotions. The ISFJ will therefore:

- Seek to develop a realistic understanding of the world as it is, in the light of what he/she observes
- Be pragmatic in nature, constantly learning to adapt to the world as it is now
- Observe in a subjective way, selecting and relating facts that others would not, and seeing those facts more in terms of impressions and significance than pure fact

The Sensing function is primarily supported by extroverted Feeling judgment—Feeling judgment is used primarily to manage the outer world of actions and spoken words. This will modify the way that the Sensing is directed by:

- Focusing the Sensing (inner world) on ideas and possibilities that relate to people
- Expressing appreciation for the contributions of others, particularly where they have done or said something that the ISFJ sees as significant
- Making decisions on the basis of values that support the ISFJ's understanding of the world
- Reinforcing the subjectivity of observation

The classic temperament of an ISFJ is Epimethean, or melancholic, for whom a basic driving force is duty, service, and the need to belong.

The INFJ
Introverted Intuition aided by Feeling

INFJs generally look to focus on possibilities, think in terms of values, and typically make decisions easily. The small number of this type (2%) is regrettable since INFJs have unusually strong drive to contribute to the welfare of others and genuinely enjoy helping their fellow men. This type can usually readily understand and deal with complex issues and people.

INFJs take their work seriously and enjoy academic activity. However, they can exhibit qualities of over perfectionism and put more into a task than perhaps is justified or demanded. They generally will not be visible leaders, but will quietly exert influence behind the scenes.

INFJs are hard to get to know. They have an unusually rich inner life, but they are reserved and tend not to share their reactions except with those they trust. Because of their vulnerability through a strong facility to interject, INFJs can be hurt rather easily by others, which, perhaps, is at least one reason they tend to be private people. People who have known an INFJ for years might find sides of their personality emerge that come as a surprise. This is not to say that INFJs are inconsistent; on the contrary, they are very consistent and value integrity.

What Makes an INFJ Tick?

The dominant function is the perceptive one of iNtuition. Characteristics associated with this function include the following:

- Likes looking at information from a global viewpoint, spotting patterns and relationships that lead to an understanding of the key issues
- Focuses more on possibilities for the future than the here-and-now
- Enjoys change, challenge, and variety

The perceptive iNtuition function is introverted. That is, iNtuition is used primarily to govern the inner world of thoughts and emotions. The INFJ will therefore:

- Seek to develop an understanding of how the world is, or can be
- Seek to understand the patterns underlying his/her observations
- Be strategic in nature, wanting to establish a clear vision toward which the INFJ is working
- Not involve others in the development of that vision

The iNtuition function is primarily supported by the extroverted Feeling judgment—Feeling judgment is used primarily to manage the outer world of actions and spoken words. This will modify the way that the iNtuition is directed by:

- Focusing the iNtuition (inner world) on ideas and possibilities that relate to people
- Expressing appreciation for the contributions of others, particularly where they have done or said something that supports the INFJ's ideals
- Making decisions on the basis of values that support the INFJ's understanding of the world, and conform to his/her vision

The classic temperament of an INFJ is Apollonian, or Choleric, for whom a basic driving force is the search for meaning or purpose.

The ENFJ
Extroverted Feeling aided by Intuition

ENFJs are often effective group leaders. They typically take it for granted that they will be followed, never doubting that people will want to do what they suggest. And, more often than not, people do, because this type has unusual charisma. ENFJs place a high value on cooperation from others and are most willing to cooperate themselves.

Found in only 5% of the general population, ENFJs place people as being of highest importance and priority. As a result, ENFJs might find themselves feeling responsible for the feelings of others to an extent, which places a burden on the relationship. An ENFJ communicates caring, concern, and a willingness to become involved. Thus people turn to ENFJs for nurture and support, which an ENFJ is usually able to deliver. At times, however, these kinds of demands can overwhelm ENFJs, who can find that they lack the skills to dissociate. ENFJs do not seem able to turn away from these demands even when they become unreasonable.

What Makes an ENFJ Tick?

The dominant function is the judging one of Feeling. Characteristics associated with this function include the following:

- Makes decisions on the basis of personal values
- Is appreciative and accepting of people—enjoying company and seeking harmony
- Assesses the impact of decisions on others by being sympathetic or compassionate
- Takes a personal approach

The judging Feeling function is extroverted. That is, Feeling is used primarily to govern the outer world of actions and spoken words. The ENFJ will therefore:

- Seek stable, harmonious relationships
- Tend to adapt to the environment, taking on board those values that are held as important by friends and family, or society as a whole
- Express the appreciation that is felt toward others
- Tend to consider others' feelings before his/her own
- Be sensitive to praise and criticism, and seek to conform to others' reasonable expectations

The Feeling function is primarily supported by the introverted iNtuitive perception—iNtuitive perception is used primarily to manage the inner world of thoughts and emotions. This will modify the way that the Feeling is directed by:

- Focusing the Feeling (outer world) on ideas and possibilities for people
- Looking for meaningful relationships
- Aiming to understand people, gaining insight into their personality and motivation

The classic temperament of an ENFJ is Apollonian, or Choleric, for whom a basic driving force is the search for meaning or purpose.

The ENFP
Extroverted Intuition aided by Feeling

For ENFPs, nothing occurs that does not have some significance, and they have an uncanny sense for the motivations of others. This gives them a talent for seeing life as an exciting drama, full of possibilities. This type is found in only about 7% of the general population, but they have great influence because of their extraordinary impact on others.

ENFPs are keen and penetrating observers and are capable of intense concentration while still being aware of what is going on about them. Their attention is never passive or casual, never wandering, but always directed. However, while ENFPs are perceptive, they can make serious mistakes in judgment. These mistakes derive from their tendency to focus on data that confirm their own biases.

ENFPs enjoy the process of creating something—an idea or a project—but are far less interested in the follow-through. They are typically enthusiastic, and this is contagious. People get caught up and entranced by an ENFP.

ENFPs are characteristically optimistic and are surprised when people or events do not turn out as anticipated.

What Makes an ENFP Tick?

The dominant function is the perceptive one of iNtuition. Characteristics associated with this function include the following:

- Likes looking at information from a global viewpoint, spotting patterns and relationships that lead to an understanding of the key issues
- Focuses more on possibilities for the future than the here-and-now
- Enjoys change, challenge, and variety

The perceptive iNtuition function is extroverted—iNtuition is used primarily to govern the outer world of actions and spoken words. The ENFP will therefore:

- Try ideas out to explore new possibilities and discover, by experience, which ones work
- Change procedures to see if any improvement can be made, rather than just continue to follow them
- Be interested in evolutionary development, but with an eye on the strategy
- Be more interested in exploring ideas than bringing them to closure

The iNtuition function is primarily supported by the introverted Feeling judgment—Feeling judgment is used primarily to manage the inner world of thoughts and emotions. This will modify the way that the iNtuition is directed by:

- Focusing the iNtuition (outer world) on ideas and possibilities that relate to people
- Inwardly appreciating the contributions of others, though not expressing it that often
- Internally rejecting any options that clearly conflict with the ENFP's values—though the rejection might not be expressed to or seen by others

The classic temperament of an ENFP is Apollonian, or Choleric, for whom a basic driving force is the search for meaning or purpose.

The INFP

Introverted Feeling aided by Intuition

INFPs present a calm, pleasant face to the world and are seen as reticent and even shy. Although they demonstrate a cool reserve toward others, inside they are anything but distant. They have a capacity for caring that is not always found in other types.

They care deeply—indeed, passionately—about a few special persons or a cause. One word that captures this type is idealistic. At times, this characteristic leaves them feeling isolated, especially since INFPs are found in only 2% of the general population. INFPs have a profound sense of honor derived from internal values. The INFP is the "defender of the Faith" or the "guardian of the castle." To understand INFPs, their cause must be understood, for they are willing to make unusual sacrifices for someone or something in which they believe.

What Makes an INFP Tick?

The dominant function is the judging one of Feeling. Characteristics associated with this function include the following:

- Makes decisions on the basis of personal values
- Is appreciative and accepting of people—enjoying company and seeking harmony
- Assesses the impact of decisions on others, being sympathetic or compassionate
- Takes a personal approach

The judging Feeling function is introverted—Feeling is used primarily to govern the inner world of thoughts and emotions. The INFP will therefore:

- Develop an inner emotional life that is often unseen to others, but is experienced as intense
- Retain a strong sense of values that are often not expressed
- Emotionally accept or reject various aspects of life—for example, deciding whether praise or criticism received is valid and, at an extreme, ignoring whatever is unacceptable to him or her
- Feel appreciation toward others, but not express it

The Feeling function is primarily supported by extroverted iNtuitive perception—iNtuitive perception is used primarily to manage the outer world of actions and spoken words. This will modify the way that the Feeling is directed by:

- Focusing the Feeling (inner world) on ideas and possibilities for people
- Looking for meaningful relationships
- Deciding on friendships through insight into their personality and motivation

The classic temperament of an INFP is Apollonian, or Choleric, for whom a basic driving force is the search for meaning or purpose.

The INTJ

Introverted Intuition aided by Thinking

INTJs are highly self-confident types, having "self-power" awareness. Found in about 1% of the general population, the INTJs live in an introspective reality, focusing on possibilities, using thinking in the form of empirical logic, and preferring that events and people serve some positive use. Decisions come naturally to INTJs, but once a decision is made, INTJs are at rest. INTJs look to the future rather than the past, and a word that captures the essence of INTJs is *builder*—a builder of systems and the applier of theoretical models.

To INTJs, authority based on position, rank, title, or publication has absolutely no force. This type is not likely to succumb to the magic of slogans, watchwords, or shibboleths. If an idea or position makes sense to an INTJ, it will be adopted; if it doesn't, it won't, regardless of who took the position or generated the idea. As with the INTP, authority per se does not impress the INTJ. INTJs do, however, tend to conform to rules if they are useful, not because they believe in them, or because they make sense, but because of their unique view of reality.

What Makes an INTJ Tick?

The dominant function is the perceptive one of iNtuition. Characteristics associated with this function include the following:

- Likes looking at information from a global viewpoint, spotting patterns and relationships that lead to an understanding of the key issues
- Focuses more on possibilities for the future than the here-and-now
- Enjoys change, challenge, and variety

The perceptive iNtuition function is introverted. That is, iNtuition is used primarily to govern the inner world of thoughts and emotions. The INTJ will therefore:

- Seek to develop an understanding of how the world can be
- Seek to understand the patterns underlying his/her observations
- Be strategic in nature, wanting to establish a clear vision toward which the INTJ is working
- Not involve others in the development of that vision

The iNtuition function is primarily supported by extroverted Thinking judgment—Thinking judgment is used primarily to manage the outer world of actions and words. This will modify the way that the iNtuition is directed by:

- Focusing the iNtuition (inner world) on ideas and possibilities that relate to systems and concepts
- Inwardly maintaining a long-term vision. Rather than communicating this vision directly, it might tend to surface in the form of criticism of ideas and situations that do not conform.
- Applying logical analysis to perceived patterns and possibilities, enabling the INTJ to quickly see the underlying principles in a situation

The classic temperament of an INTJ is Promethean, or Phlegmatic, for whom a basic driving force is the search for competence or excellence.

The ENTJ

Extroverted Thinking aided by Intuition

If one word were used to capture ENTJ's style, it would be *commander.* The basic driving force and need of ENTJs is to lead, and from an early age, they can be observed taking over groups. This type is found in approximately 5% of the total population.

ENTJs have a strong urge to give structure wherever they are—to harness people to achieve particular goals. Their empirical, objective, and extroverted thinking is typically highly developed; if this is the case, they use classification, generalization, summarization, and demonstration of what is required in simple language with ease. They resemble ESTJs in their tendency to establish plans for a task, enterprise, or organization, but an ENTJ's search is more for policy and goals than for regulations and procedures. An ENTJ's introverted thinking (analysis and conservation) may be less well developed than the extroverted thinking processes, and the ENTJ leader might turn to an ENTP or INTP to provide this kind of input.

What Makes an ENTJ Tick?

The dominant function is the judging one of Thinking. Characteristics associated with this function include the following:

- Likes making decisions on the basis of logic, using objective considerations
- Is concerned with truth, principles, and justice
- Is analytical and critical, tending to see the flaws in situations
- Takes an objective approach

The judging Thinking function is extroverted—Thinking is used primarily to govern the outer world of actions and spoken words. The ENTJ will therefore:

- Organize life on a logical basis, classifying, ordering, and directing facts and situations
- Be decisive, with the aim of being just and fair
- Spontaneously criticize
- Be comfortable with conflict as a way of resolving problems
- Take an impersonal approach, focusing more on systems and organizational needs than on each individual's feelings

The Thinking function is primarily supported by the introverted iNtuitive perception—iNtuitive perception is used primarily to manage the inner world of thoughts and emotions. This will modify the way that the Thinking is directed by:

- Focusing the Thinking (outer world) on creative decisions that lead to change and new possibilities
- Orchestrating the outward organization in support of some overall purpose or strategy

The classic temperament of an ENTJ is Promethean, or Phlegmatic, for whom a basic driving force is the search for competence or excellence.

The ENTP
Extroverted Intuition aided by Thinking

ENTPs like to exercise their ingenuity in the world of people and things. Found in about five out of every hundred people, ENTPs often deal imaginatively with social relationships as well as physical and mechanical relations. They are very alert to what is apt to occur next, and always sensitive to possibilities.

ENTPs are usually good at analysis, especially functional analysis, and have both a tolerance for and enjoyment of the complex. Usually enthusiastic, ENTPs are apt to express interest in everything, and thus can be a source of inspiration to others who find themselves caught up by the ENTP's enthusiasm. This type is delighted over many things and is therefore easy to please, often showing the effervescence of their NF counterpart, the ENFP. The ENTP is the most reluctant of all the types to do things in a particular manner just because that is the way things always have been done. They characteristically have an eye out for a better way, always on the lookout for new projects, new activities, and new procedures.

The ENTP can be an entrepreneur and makes do with whatever or whoever is at hand, counting on ingenuity to solve problems as they arise, rather than carefully generating a detailed blueprint in advance. A rough draft is all that an ENTP needs to feel confident and ready to proceed into action, counting on the ability to improvise as a situation develops.

What Makes an ENTP Tick?

The dominant function is the perceptive one of iNtuition. Characteristics associated with this function include the following:

- Likes looking at information from a global viewpoint, spotting patterns and relationships that lead to an understanding of the key issues
- Focuses more on possibilities for the future than the here-and-now
- Enjoys change, challenge, and variety

The perceptive iNtuition function is extroverted. That is, iNtuition is used primarily to govern the outer world of actions and spoken words. The ENTP will therefore:

- Try ideas out to explore new possibilities and discover, by experience, which ones work
- Change procedures to see if any improvement can be made, rather than just continue to follow them
- Be interested primarily in evolutionary development, perhaps with an eye on the strategy
- Be more interested in exploring ideas than bringing them to closure

The iNtuition function is primarily supported by the introverted Thinking judgment—Thinking judgment is used primarily to manage the inner world of thoughts and emotions. This will modify the way that the iNtuition is directed by:

- Focusing the iNtuition (outer world) on ideas and possibilities that relate to systems and concepts
- Inwardly tending to spot the flaws in situations, people, or ideas; rather than expressing criticism directly, it may surface in the form of contradictory ideas and possibilities
- Applying logical analysis to perceived patterns and possibilities, enabling the ENTP to quickly see the underlying principles in a situation

The classic temperament of an ENTP is Promethean, or Phlegmatic, for whom a basic driving force is the search for competence or excellence.

The INTP
Introverted Thinking aided by Intuition

INTPs exhibit the greatest precision in thought and language of all the types; they tend to see distinctions and inconsistencies in thought and language instantaneously. The one word that captures the unique style of INTPs is architect—the architect of ideas and systems as well as the architect of edifices. This type is found in only 3% of the population and therefore is not encountered as frequently as some of the other types.

INTPs abhor redundancy and incoherence. Possessing a desire to understand the universe, an INTP is constantly looking for natural law. Curiosity concerning these keys to the universe is a driving force.

INTPs prize intelligence in themselves and in others, but can become intellectual dilettantes as a result of their need to amass ideas, principles, or understanding of behavior. And once they know something, it is remembered. INTPs can become obsessed with analysis. Once caught up in a thought process, INTPs are consumed and persevere until the issue is comprehended in all its complexity. They can be intellectual snobs and might show impatience at times with others less endowed intellectually. This quality, INTPs find, generates hostility and defensive behavior on the part of others who might describe an INTP as being arrogant.

What Makes an INTP Tick?

The dominant function is the judging one of Thinking. Characteristics associated with this function include the following:

- Likes making decisions on the basis of logic, using objective considerations
- Is concerned with truth, principles, and justice
- Is analytical and critical, tending to see the flaws in situations
- Takes an objective approach

The judging Thinking function is introverted. That is, Thinking is used primarily to govern the inner world of thoughts and emotions. The INTP will therefore:

- Spend time thinking analytically, organizing thoughts on a logical basis
- Develop an understanding of the principles involved in a situation
- Spontaneously feel critical of a person or situation, but not necessarily express that criticism
- Be inwardly decisive, but not communicate those decisions to others
- Think mostly about impersonal issues, focusing more on concepts, truths, and systems rather than individuals' feelings

The Thinking function is primarily supported by the extroverted iNtuitive perception—the iNtuitive perception is used primarily to manage the outer world of actions and spoken words. This will modify the way that the Thinking is directed by:

- Focusing the Thinking (inner world) on understanding possibilities for the future
- Perceiving patterns in information to support the logical analysis

The classic temperament of an INTP is Promethean, or Phlegmatic, for whom a basic driving force is the search for competence or excellence.

Understanding the Psychological Types Code

The following hierarchical diagram represents a simple but useful way to understand the way that the 16 psychological types are described by the letters in Jung's cognitive processes.

1. Write your type into the four blank boxes at the top of the diagram.
2. Look at the last letter in the code. It tells you which of the two middle letters is extroverted—if it is J, then the T or F (the third letter) in the code is used in the external world. If it is P, then the S or N (the second letter) in the code is used in the external world.
3. Once you have determined which process is extroverted, you can now determine that the remaining middle letter in the code is introverted.
4. Look at the first letter in the code. If it is an "E," then the extroverted process identified in step two is the dominant process. If it is an "I," then the introverted process identified in step two is the dominant process.
5. The remaining middle letter is the supporting or auxiliary process.

Jung's Cognitive processes as they appear in the four-letter Personality Type Code

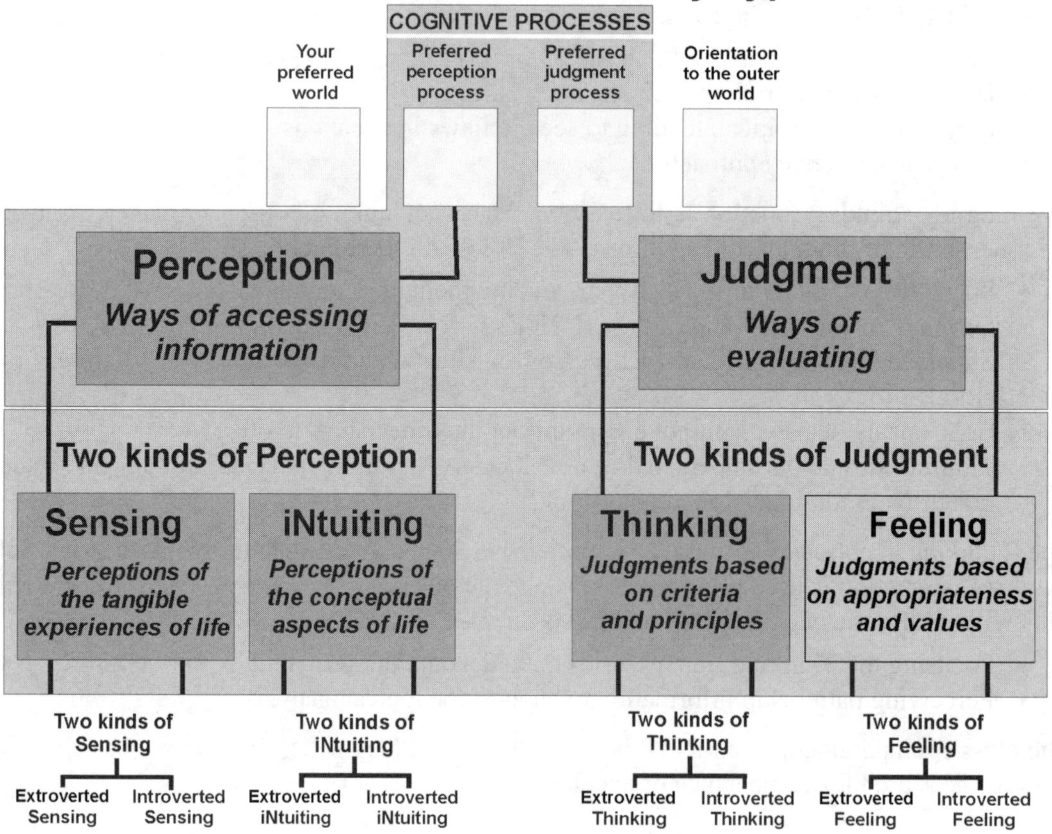